I0426261

June 2012

DOD BUSINESS SYSTEMS MODERNIZATION

Governance Mechanisms for Implementing Management Controls Need to Be Improved

GAO
Accountability ★ Integrity ★ Reliability

DOD BUSINESS SYSTEMS MODERNIZATION

Governance Mechanisms for Implementing Management Controls Need to Be Improved

Highlights of GAO-12-685, a report to congressional committees

Why GAO Did This Study

For decades, DOD has been challenged in modernizing its business systems. Since 1995, GAO has designated DOD's business systems modernization program as high risk, and it continues to do so today. To assist in addressing DOD's business system modernization challenges, the National Defense Authorization Act for Fiscal Year 2005 requires the department to take certain actions prior to obligating funds for covered systems. It also requires DOD to annually report to the congressional defense committees on these actions and for GAO to review each annual report. In response, GAO performed its annual review of DOD's actions to comply with the act and related federal guidance. To do so, GAO reviewed, for example, the latest version of DOD's business enterprise architecture, fiscal year 2013 budget submission, investment management policies and procedures, and certification actions for its business system investments.

What GAO Recommends

GAO recommends that the Secretary of Defense take steps to strengthen the department's mechanisms for governing its business systems modernization activities. DOD concurred with two of GAO's recommendations and partially concurred with one, but did not concur with the recommendation that it report progress on staffing the office responsible for business systems modernization to the congressional defense committees. GAO maintains that including staffing progress information in DOD's annual report will facilitate congressional oversight and promote departmental accountability.

View GAO-12-685. For more information, contact Valerie Melvin at (202) 512-6304 or melvinv@gao.gov.

What GAO Found

The Department of Defense (DOD) continues to take steps to comply with the provisions of the Ronald W. Reagan National Defense Authorization Act for Fiscal Year 2005, as amended, and to satisfy relevant system modernization management guidance. While the department has initiated numerous activities aimed at addressing the act, it has been limited in its ability to demonstrate results. Specifically, the department

- released its most recent business enterprise architecture version, which continues to address the act's requirements and is consistent with the department's future vision for developing its architecture. However, the architecture has not yet resulted in a streamlined and modernized business systems environment, in part, because DOD has not fully defined the roles, responsibilities, and relationships associated with developing and implementing the architecture.
- included a range of information for 1,657 business system investments in its fiscal year 2013 budget submission; however, it does not reflect about 500 business systems, due in part to the lack of a reliable, comprehensive inventory of all defense business systems.
- has not implemented key practices from GAO's Information Technology Investment Management framework since GAO's last review in 2011. In addition, while DOD has reported its intent to implement a new organizational structure and guidance to address statutory requirements, this structure and guidance have yet to be established. Further, DOD has begun to implement a business process reengineering review process but has not yet measured and reported results.
- continues to describe certification actions in its annual report for its business system investments as required by the act—DOD approved 198 actions to certify, decertify, or recertify defense business system modernizations, which represented a total of $2.2 billion in modernization spending. However, the basis for these actions and subsequent approvals is supported with limited information, such as unvalidated architectural compliance assertions.
- lacks the full complement of staff it identified as needed to perform business systems modernization responsibilities. Specifically, the office of the Deputy Chief Management Officer, which took over these responsibilities from another office in September 2011, reported that 41 percent of its positions were unfilled.

DOD's progress in modernizing its business systems is limited, in part, by continued uncertainty surrounding the department's governance mechanisms, such as roles and responsibilities of key organizations and senior leadership positions. Until DOD fully implements governance mechanisms to address these long-standing institutional modernization management controls provided for under the act, addressed in GAO recommendations, and otherwise embodied in relevant guidance; its business systems modernization will likely remain a high-risk program.

Contents

Abbreviations

CIO	Chief Information Officer
BEA	business enterprise architecture
BPR	business process reengineering
DCMO	Deputy Chief Management Officer
DITPR	Defense Information Technology Portfolio Repository
DOD	Department of Defense
DON	Department of the Navy
IRB	investment review board
IT	information technology
ITIM	Information Technology Investment Management
NDAA	National Defense Authorization Act
SNAP-IT	Select and Native Programming Data Input System—Information Technology

United States Government Accountability Office
Washington, DC 20548

June 1, 2012

Congressional Committees

For decades, the Department of Defense (DOD) has been challenged in modernizing its business systems. In 1995, we designated the department's business systems modernization program as high risk because of its vulnerability to fraud, waste, abuse, and mismanagement, and because of opportunities to achieve greater efficiencies and free up resources for higher-priority needs; and we continue to designate it as such today.[1] In addition, we have reported that significant potential exists for identifying and avoiding costs associated with duplicative functionality across these business system investments,[2] which account for billions of dollars in annual expenditures and, according to the department, include about 2,200 systems. Moreover, the systems that comprise DOD's business systems environment contribute to many DOD initiatives, including improving departmentwide financial management and military personnel health care.

---

[1]GAO, *High-Risk Series: An Update*, GAO-11-278 (Washington, D.C.: February 2011).

[2]GAO, *Opportunities to Reduce Potential Duplication in Government Programs, Save Tax Dollars, and Enhance Revenue*, GAO-11-318SP (Washington, D.C.: Mar. 1, 2011) and *Follow-up on 2011 Report: Status of Actions Taken to Reduce Duplication, Overlap, and Fragmentation, Save Tax Dollars, and Enhance Revenue*, GAO-12-453SP (Washington, D.C.: Feb. 28, 2012).

Since May 2001, we have recommended[3] that the Secretary of Defense establish the means for effectively developing an enterprise architecture and a corporate, architecture-centric approach to investment control and decision making—two essential ingredients to a successful systems modernization program.[4] Further, Congress has included provisions in the Ronald W. Reagan National Defense Authorization Act (NDAA) for Fiscal Year 2005,[5] as amended, that were consistent with our recommendations. More specifically, section 332 of the act, as amended, requires the department to, among other things, (1) develop a business enterprise architecture (BEA) and a transition plan for implementing the architecture, (2) identify systems information in its annual budget submission, (3) establish a systems investment approval and accountability structure along with an investment review process, and (4) certify and approve any business system program costing in excess of $1 million. The act further requires that the Secretary of Defense submit an annual report to the congressional defense committees on DOD's

---

[3]GAO, *DOD Business Systems Modernization: Long-standing Weaknesses in Enterprise Architecture Development Need to Be Addressed*, GAO-05-702 (Washington, D.C.: July 22, 2005); *DOD Business Systems Modernization: Billions Being Invested without Adequate Oversight*, GAO-05-381 (Washington, D.C.: Apr. 29, 2005); *DOD Business Systems Modernization: Limited Progress in Development of Business Enterprise Architecture and Oversight of Information Technology Investments*, GAO-04-731R (Washington, D.C.: May 17, 2004); *DOD Business Systems Modernization: Important Progress Made to Develop Business Enterprise Architecture, but Much Work Remains*, GAO-03-1018 (Washington, D.C.: Sept. 19, 2003); *Business Systems Modernization: Summary of GAO's Assessment of the Department of Defense's Initial Business Enterprise Architecture*, GAO-03-877R (Washington, D.C.: July 7, 2003); *Information Technology: Observations on Department of Defense's Draft Enterprise Architecture*, GAO-03-571R (Washington, D.C.: Mar. 28, 2003); *DOD Business Systems Modernization: Improvements to Enterprise Architecture Development and Implementation Efforts Needed*, GAO-03-458 (Washington, D.C.: Feb. 28, 2003); and *Information Technology: Architecture Needed to Guide Modernization of DOD's Financial Operations*, GAO-01-525 (Washington, D.C.: May 17, 2001).

[4]An enterprise architecture, or modernization blueprint, provides a clear and comprehensive picture of an entity, whether it is an organization (e.g., federal department or agency) or a functional or mission area that cuts across more than one organization (e.g., financial management). This picture consists of snapshots of the enterprise's current or "as-is" operational and technological environment and its target or "to-be" environment, and contains a capital investment road map for transitioning from the current to the target environment. These snapshots consist of "views," which are basically one or more architecture products that provide conceptual or logical representations of the enterprise.

[5]Pub. L. No. 108-375, § 332, 118 Stat. 1811, 1851-1856 (Oct. 28, 2004) (codified in part at 10 U.S.C. § 2222. Hereafter, we refer to the provisions of 10 U.S.C. § 2222, including its amendments, as 'the act.').

compliance with certain requirements of the act not later than March 15 of each year, through 2016. Additionally, the act directed us to submit to these congressional committees—within 60 days of DOD's report submission—an assessment of the department's actions to comply with the requirements of the act.

As agreed with your offices, the objective of our review was to assess the actions by DOD to comply with the act and related federal guidance. To address the enterprise architecture and investment management provisions, we focused on progress that has been made relative to developing the federated BEA[6] and establishing investment management structures and processes, using our prior reports as a baseline.[7] To address the budgetary disclosure and certification provisions of the act, we reviewed the department's report to Congress, which was submitted on April 3, 2012, and evaluated the information used to satisfy the budget submission and investment review, certification, and approval aspects of the act. We did not evaluate the department's updated enterprise transition plan because an updated plan was not issued during the time period covered by our audit.

We conducted this performance audit at DOD and military department offices in Arlington and Alexandria, VA, from September 2011 to June 2012 in accordance with generally accepted government auditing standards. Those standards require that we plan and perform the audit to obtain sufficient, appropriate evidence to provide a reasonable basis for

---

[6]Under a federated enterprise architecture approach, certain rules, policies, procedures, and services are defined by higher-level architectures and apply to subordinate architectures, which are substantially autonomous.

[7]GAO, *Department of Defense: Further Actions Needed to Institutionalize Key Business System Modernization Management Controls*, GAO-11-684 (Washington, D.C.: June 29, 2011); *Business Systems Modernization: Scope and Content of DOD's Congressional Report and Executive Oversight of Investments Need to Improve*, GAO-10-663 (Washington, D.C.: May 24, 2010); *DOD Business Systems Modernization: Recent Slowdown in Institutionalizing Key Management Controls Needs to Be Addressed*, GAO-09-586 (Washington, D.C.: May 18, 2009); *DOD Business Systems Modernization: Military Departments Need to Strengthen Management of Enterprise Architecture Programs*, GAO-08-519 (Washington, D.C.: May 12, 2008); *Business Systems Modernization: Department of the Navy Needs to Establish Management Structure and Fully Define Policies and Procedures for Institutionally Managing Investments*, GAO-08-53 (Washington, D.C.: Oct. 31, 2007); and *Business Systems Modernization: Air Force Needs to Fully Define Policies and Procedures for Institutionally Managing Investments*, GAO-08-52 (Washington, D.C.: Oct. 31, 2007).

our findings and conclusions based on our audit objectives. We believe that the evidence obtained provides a reasonable basis for our findings and conclusions based on our audit objectives. Details on our objective, scope, and methodology are contained in appendix I.

Background

DOD is one of the largest and most complex organizations in the world, and is entrusted with more taxpayer dollars than any other federal department or agency. For fiscal year 2013, the department requested approximately $613.9 billion—$525.4 billion in spending authority for its base operations and an additional $88.5 billion to support overseas contingency operations, such as those in Iraq and Afghanistan.

In support of its military operations, DOD performs an assortment of interrelated and interdependent business functions, such as logistics management, procurement, health care management, and financial management. As we have previously reported, the DOD systems environment that supports these business functions is overly complex and error prone, and is characterized by (1) little standardization across the department, (2) multiple systems performing the same tasks, (3) the same data stored in multiple systems, and (4) the need for data to be entered manually into multiple systems.[8] The department recently requested about $17.2 billion for its business systems environment and IT infrastructure investments for fiscal year 2013.[9] According to the department's systems inventory, this environment is composed of about 2,200 business systems and includes 310 financial management, 724 human resource management, 580 logistics, 254 real property and installation, and 287 weapon acquisition management systems.

DOD currently bears responsibility, in whole or in part, for 14 of the 30 areas across the federal government that we have designated as high

---

[8]GAO, *DOD Financial Management: Implementation Weaknesses in Army and Air Force Business Systems Could Jeopardize DOD's Auditability Goals,* GAO-12-134 (Washington, D.C.: Feb. 28, 2012).

[9]This figure reflects DOD's unclassified budget request for all systems not considered national security systems.

risk.[10] Seven of these areas are specific to the department,[11] and 7 other high-risk areas are shared with other federal agencies.[12] Collectively, these high-risk areas relate to DOD's major business operations that are inextricably linked to the department's ability to perform its overall mission. Furthermore, the high-risk areas directly affect the readiness and capabilities of U.S. military forces and can affect the success of a mission. In particular, the department's nonintegrated and duplicative systems impair its ability to combat fraud, waste, and abuse.[13] As such, DOD's business systems modernization is one of the department's specific high-risk areas and is an essential enabler in addressing many of the department's other high-risk areas. For example, modernized business systems are integral to the department's efforts to address its financial, supply chain, and information security management high-risk areas.

DOD's Approach to Business Systems Modernization

The department's approach to modernizing its business systems environment includes developing and using a BEA and associated enterprise transition plan, improving business systems investment management, and reengineering the business processes supported by its defense business systems. These efforts are guided by DOD's Chief Management Officer and Deputy Chief Management Officer (DCMO). The Chief Management Officer's responsibilities include developing and maintaining a departmentwide strategic plan for business reform and

---

[10]GAO-11-278.

[11]These seven high-risk areas include DOD's overall approach to business transformation, business systems modernization, contract management, financial management, supply chain management, support infrastructure management, and weapon systems acquisition.

[12]The seven governmentwide high-risk areas include disability programs, ensuring the effective protection of technologies critical to U.S. national security interests, interagency contracting, information systems and critical infrastructure, information sharing for homeland security, human capital, and real property.

[13]GAO, *DOD Business Systems Modernization: Planned Investment in Navy Program to Create Cashless Shipboard Environment Needs to Be Justified and Better Managed*, GAO-08-922 (Washington, D.C.: Sept. 8, 2008); *DOD Travel Cards: Control Weaknesses Resulted in Millions of Dollars of Improper Payments*, GAO-04-576 (Washington, D.C.: June 9, 2004); *Military Pay: Army National Guard Personnel Mobilized to Active Duty Experienced Significant Pay Problems*, GAO-04-89 (Washington, D.C.: Nov. 13, 2003); and *Defense Inventory: Opportunities Exist to Improve Spare Parts Support Aboard Deployed Navy Ships*, GAO-03-887 (Washington, D.C.: Aug. 29, 2003).

establishing performance goals and measures for improving and evaluating overall economy, efficiency, and effectiveness, and monitoring and measuring the progress of the department. The DCMO's responsibilities include recommending to the Chief Management Officer methodologies and measurement criteria to better synchronize, integrate, and coordinate the business operations to ensure alignment in support of the warfighting mission. The DCMO is also responsible for developing and maintaining the department's enterprise architecture for its business mission area.[14]

The DOD Chief Management Officer and DCMO are to interact with several entities to guide the direction, oversight, and execution of DOD's business transformation efforts, which include business systems modernization. These entities include the Defense Business Systems Management Committee, which is intended to serve as the department's highest-ranking investment review and decision-making body for business systems programs and is chaired by the Deputy Secretary of Defense. The committee's composition includes the principal staff assistants, defense agency directors, DOD Chief Information Officer (CIO), and military department Chief Management Officers. Table 1 describes key DOD business systems modernization governance entities and their composition.

---

[14]According to DOD, the business mission area is responsible for ensuring that capabilities, resources, and materiel are reliably delivered to the warfighter. Specifically, the business mission area addresses areas such as real property and human resources management.

Table 1: DOD Business Systems Modernization Governance Entities' Selected Roles, Responsibilities, and Composition

Entity	Roles and responsibilities	Composition
Defense Business Systems Management Committee	Provide strategic direction and plans for the business mission area in coordination with the warfighting and enterprise information environment mission areas. Recommend policies and procedures required to integrate DOD business transformation and attain cross-department, end-to-end interoperability of business systems and processes. Serve as approving authority for business system modernizations greater than $1 million. Establish policies and approve the business mission area strategic plan, the enterprise transition plan for implementation of business systems modernization, and the BEA.	Chaired by the Deputy Secretary of Defense/Chief Management Officer; the Vice Chair is the DCMO. Includes senior leadership in the Office of the Secretary of Defense, such as the DOD CIO. Also includes the military department Chief Management Officers, the heads of select defense agencies, and other senior participation by the Joint Chiefs of Staff and the U.S. Transportation Command.
Principal Staff Assistants/Certification Authorities	Support the Defense Business Systems Management Committee's management of enterprise business IT investments. Serve as the certification authorities accountable for the obligation of funds for respective business system modernizations within designated core business missions.[a] Review, approve, and oversee the planning, design, acquisition, deployment, operation, maintenance, and modernization of the defense business systems assigned. Provide the Defense Business Systems Management Committee with recommendations for system investment approval. Provide input into enterprise-level architecture products and transition plans that support their core business mission.	Composed of the Under Secretaries of Defense for Acquisition, Technology, and Logistics; Comptroller; and Personnel and Readiness; DOD CIO; and the Deputy Secretary of Defense.
Investment Review Boards (IRB)	Serve as the oversight and investment decision-making bodies for those business capabilities that support activities under their designated areas of responsibility. Review and recommend certification for all business systems modernization investments costing more than $1 million that are integrated and compliant with the BEA.	Includes the principal staff assistants, Joint Staff, DOD CIO, core business mission area representatives, military departments, defense agencies, and combatant commands.
Precertification Authority[b]	Ensures component-level investment review processes integrate with the investment management system. Identifies those component systems that require IRB certification and prepare, review, approve, validate, and transfer investment documentation as required. Assesses and precertifies business process reengineering efforts and architecture compliance of component systems submitted for certification and annual review.	Includes the Chief Management Officer from Air Force, the Army, the Navy, and the DOD DCMO representing the defense agencies or a business system supported by more than one military department or defense agency.

GAO-12-685 DOD Business Systems Modernization

Entity	Roles and responsibilities	Composition
Office of the DCMO	Maintains and updates the department's BEA and enterprise transition plan. Ensures that functional priorities and requirements of various defense components, such as the Army and the Defense Logistics Agency, are reflected in the architecture. Ensures adoption of departmentwide information and process standards as defined in the architecture. Serves as the day-to-day management entity of the business transformation effort at the DOD enterprise level.	Composed of six directorates (Investment and Acquisition Management; Business Integration; Technology, Innovation, and Engineering; Planning and Performance Management; Expeditionary Business Operations; and Operations).

Source: GAO analysis of DOD information.

Note: This table reflects DOD's current approach. As described in this report, DOD is taking steps to revise this approach consistent with changes required by the NDAA for Fiscal Year 2012.

[a]DOD has five core business missions: Human Resources Management, Weapon Systems Lifecycle Management, Materiel Supply and Service Management, Real Property and Installations Lifecycle Management, and Financial Management.

[b]In the military departments, the Chief Management Officer is the precertification authority. For the defense agencies, precertification activities are performed by the component, and the DCMO is the precertification authority. These precertification activities result in a Chief Management Officer Determination Memorandum.

Overview of DOD's Tiered Accountability for Business Systems Modernization

Since 2005, DOD has employed a "tiered accountability" approach to business systems modernization. Under this approach, responsibility and accountability for business architectures and systems investment management are assigned to different levels in the organization. For example, the DCMO is responsible for developing the corporate BEA (i.e., the thin layer of DOD-wide policies, capabilities, standards, and rules) and the associated enterprise transition plan. Each component is responsible for defining a component-level architecture and transition plan associated with its own tiers of responsibility and for doing so in a manner that is aligned with (i.e., does not violate) the corporate BEA. Similarly, program managers are responsible for developing program-level architectures and plans and for ensuring alignment with the architectures and transition plans above them. This concept is to allow for autonomy while also ensuring linkages and alignment from the program level through the component level to the corporate level.

Consistent with the tiered accountability approach, the NDAA for Fiscal Year 2008 required the Secretaries of the military departments to designate the department Under Secretaries as Chief Management

Officers with primary responsibility for business operations.[15] Moreover, the Duncan Hunter NDAA for Fiscal Year 2009 required the military departments to establish business transformation offices to assist their Chief Management Officers in the development of comprehensive business transformation plans.[16] In response, all of the military departments have designated their respective Under Secretaries as the Chief Management Officers. In addition, the Department of the Navy (DON) and Army have issued business transformation plans. Air Force officials have stated that the department's corporate Strategic Plan also serves as its business transformation plan.

DOD's Approach to Developing Its BEA

DOD's BEA is intended to serve as a blueprint for DOD business transformation. In particular, the BEA is to guide and constrain implementation of interoperable defense business systems by, among other things, documenting the department's business functions and activities, the information needed to execute its functions and activities, and the business rules, laws, regulations, and policies associated with its business functions and activities. According to DOD, the BEA is being developed using an incremental approach, where each new release addresses business mission area gaps or weaknesses based on priorities identified by the department. The department considers its current approach to developing the BEA both a "top-down" and "bottom-up" approach. Specifically, it focuses on developing content to support investment management and strategic decision making and oversight ("top-down") while also responding to department needs associated with supporting system implementation, system integration, and software development ("bottom-up").

The department's most recent BEA version (version 9.0), released in March 2012, focuses on documenting information associated with its 15 end-to-end business process areas. (See table 2 for a list and description of these business process areas.) In particular, the department's most recent Strategic Management Plan has identified the Hire-to-Retire and Procure-to-Pay business process areas as its priorities. According to the department, the process of documenting the needed architecture information also includes working to refine and streamline each of the associated end-to-end business processes.

---

[15]Pub. L. No. 110-181, § 904(b), 122 Stat. 3, 274 (Jan. 28, 2008).

[16]Pub. L. No. 110-417, § 908, 122 Stat. 4356, 4569 (Oct. 14, 2008).

Table 2: DOD's End-to-End Business Processes

Business process	Description
Acquire-to-Retire	Encompasses business functions necessary to obtain, manage and dispose of accountable and reportable property (capitalized and noncapitalized assets) through their entire life cycle.
Budget-to-Report	Encompasses business functions necessary to plan, formulate, create, execute against, and report on the budget and business activities of the entity.
Concept-to-Product	Encompasses business functions necessary to effectively identify product needs, and plan and execute all necessary activities to bring a product from initial concept to full production.
Cost Management	Encompasses business functions necessary to identify, collect, measure, accumulate, analyze, interpret, and communicate cost information to accomplish the many objectives associated with control, decision making, planning, and reporting.
Deployment-to-Redeployment/Retrograde	Encompasses all business functions necessary to plan, notify, deploy, sustain, recall, and reset tactical units to and from theaters of engagement.
Environmental Liabilities	Encompasses business functions necessary to identify environmental cleanup, closure, or disposal issues that represent an environmental liability of the department, to develop cost estimates and expenditures related to the actions required to eliminate an identified environmental liability, and to report appropriate financial information about the environmental liability.
Hire-to-Retire	Encompasses business functions necessary to plan for, hire, classify, develop, assign, track, account for, compensate, retain, and separate the persons needed to accomplish aspects of the DOD mission.
Market-to-Prospect	Encompasses business functions necessary to establish marketing plans, identify target markets, plan and define marketing campaigns, execute marketing campaigns, and measure and evaluate the performance of marketing campaigns.
Order-to-Cash	Encompasses business functions necessary to accept and process customer orders for services and/or inventory held for sale.
Plan-to-Stock	Encompasses business functions necessary to plan, procure, produce, inventory, and stock materials used both in operations and maintenance as well as for sale.
Procure-to-Pay	Encompasses business functions necessary to obtain goods and services.
Proposal-to-Reward	Encompasses the life cycle of the grant process from the grantor perspective. It includes all the business functions necessary to plan, solicit, review, award, perform, monitor, and close out a grant.
Prospect-to-Order	Encompasses business functions necessary to generate and sustain sales by pursuing qualified leads, employing effective sales techniques, efficient order processing, maintaining customer relationships and providing support functions to include service, personnel and financial impacts.
Service Request-to-Resolution	Encompasses the process of performing maintenance on materiel/assets requiring repair or complete rebuild of parts, assemblies, subassemblies, and end-items, including the manufacture of parts, modifications, testing, and reclamation as required. It also includes the process whereby buildings and other fixed facilities are maintained and renovated during their life cycle.
Service-to-Satisfaction	Encompasses all business functions necessary to determine service requirements, secure funding, contract with outside vendor, establish service and measure customer satisfaction.

Source: GAO based on DOD documentation.

In addition, DOD's approach to developing its BEA involves the development of a federated enterprise architecture. Such an approach treats the architecture as a family of coherent but distinct member architectures that conform to an overarching architectural view and rule set. This approach recognizes that each member of the federation has unique goals and needs, as well as common roles and responsibilities with the levels above and below it. Under a federated approach, member architectures are substantially autonomous, although they also inherit certain rules, policies, procedures, and services from higher-level architectures. As such, a federated architecture gives autonomy to an organization's components while ensuring enterprisewide linkages and alignment where appropriate. Where commonality among components exists, there are also opportunities for identifying and leveraging shared services. Figure 1 provides a conceptual overview of DOD's federated BEA approach.

Figure 1: Conceptual Overview of DOD's Federated BEA Approach

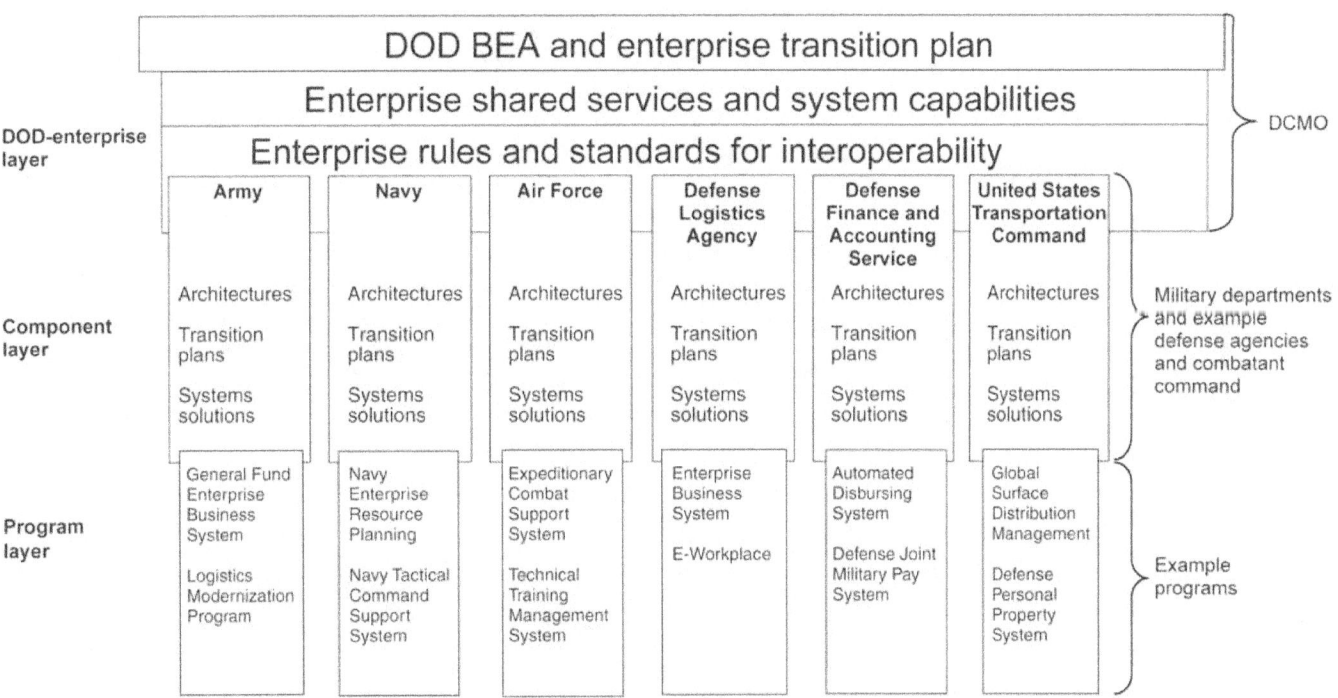

Source: GAO analysis of DOD data.

DOD's Approach to Certifying Business System Investments

The certification of business system investments is a key step in DOD's IT investment selection process that the department has aimed to model after GAO's Information Technology Investment Management (ITIM) framework.[17] While defense business systems with a total cost over $1 million are required, as of June 2011, to use the Business Capability Lifecycle,[18] a streamlined process for acquiring systems, these systems are also subject to the formal review and certification process through the IRBs before funds are obligated for them.

Under DOD's current approach to certifying investments, there are several types of certification actions as follows:

- Certify or certify with conditions: An IRB certifies the modernization as fully meeting criteria defined in the act and IRB investment review guidance (certify) or imposes specific conditions to be addressed by a certain time (certify with conditions).

- Recertify or recertify with conditions: An IRB certifies the obligation of additional modernization funds for a previously-certified modernization investment (recertify) or imposes additional related conditions to the action (recertify with conditions).

- Decertify: An IRB may decertify or reduce the amount of modernization funds available to an investment when (1) a component reduces funding for a modernization by more than 10 percent of the originally certified amount, (2) the period of certification for a modernization is shortened, or (3) the entire amount of funding is not to be obligated as previously certified. An IRB may also decertify a modernization after development has been terminated or if previous conditions assigned by the IRB are not met.

---

[17]GAO's ITIM framework provides a method for evaluating and assessing how well an agency is selecting and managing its IT resources. The framework, which describes five progressive stages of maturity that an agency can achieve in its investment management capabilities, was developed on the basis of our research into the IT investment management practices of leading private- and public-sector organizations. See GAO, *Information Technology Investment Management: A Framework for Assessing and Improving Process Maturity*, GAO-04-394G (Washington, D.C.: March 2004).

[18]The Business Capability Lifecycle is to be the overarching framework for the planning, design, acquisition, deployment, operations, maintenance, and modernization of defense business systems. It applies to any system modernization (a system increment or a complete system) with a total cost over $1 million and outlines specific timelines for development milestones. For example, when a Major Automated Information System enters the acquisition process, all functional capabilities associated with a given increment must be achievable within five years from when funds were first obligated.

Summary of NDAA Requirements

Congress included provisions in the act, as amended, that are aimed at ensuring DOD's development of a well-defined BEA and associated enterprise transition plan, as well as the establishment and implementation of effective investment management structures and processes.[19] The act requires DOD to

- develop a BEA and an enterprise transition plan for implementing the architecture,

- identify each business system proposed for funding in DOD's fiscal year budget submissions,

- delegate the responsibility for business systems to designated authorities within DOD,

- establish an investment review structure and process, and

- not obligate appropriated funds for a defense business system program with a total cost of more than $1 million unless the approval authority certifies that the business system program meets specified conditions.[20]

The act also requires that the Secretary of Defense annually submit to the congressional defense committees a report on the department's compliance with the above provisions.

In addition, the act sets forth the following responsibilities:

---

[19]10 U.S.C. § 2222.

[20]The act, as amended (10 U.S.C. § 2222(a)), requires the appropriate precertification authority to determine that a defense business system program (1) (a) is in compliance with the enterprise architecture and (b) has undertaken appropriate business process reengineering efforts; (2) is necessary to achieve a critical national security capability or address a critical requirement in an area such as safety or security; or (3) is necessary to prevent a significant adverse effect on a project that is needed to achieve an essential capability, taking into consideration the alternative solutions for preventing such an adverse effect. The NDAA for Fiscal Year 2012 requires that the certification and approval requirements apply to all business systems programs that are expected to cost over $1 million over the period of the current Future-Years Defense Program. Previously, the certification requirement only applied to business system modernizations with a total cost in excess of $1 million.

- the DCMO is responsible and accountable for developing and maintaining the BEA, as well as integrating business operations;

- the CIO is responsible and accountable for the content of those portions of the BEA that support DOD's IT infrastructure or information assurance activities;

- the Under Secretary of Defense for Acquisition, Technology, and Logistics is responsible and accountable for the content of those portions of the BEA that support DOD's acquisition, logistics, installations, environment, or safety and occupational health activities;

- the Under Secretary of Defense (Comptroller) is responsible and accountable for the content of those portions of the BEA that support DOD's financial management activities or strategic planning and budgeting activities; and

- the Under Secretary of Defense for Personnel and Readiness is responsible and accountable for the content of those portions of the BEA that support DOD's human resource management activities.

Prior GAO Reviews of DOD's Business Systems Modernization

Between 2005 and 2008, we reported that DOD had taken steps to comply with key requirements of the NDAA relative to architecture development, transition plan development, budgetary disclosure, and investment review, and to satisfy relevant systems modernization management guidance. However, each report also concluded that much remained to be accomplished relative to the act's requirements and relevant guidance.[21] We made recommendations to address each of the areas.

---

[21]GAO, *DOD Business Systems Modernization: Progress in Establishing Corporate Management Controls Needs to Be Replicated Within Military Departments,* GAO-08-705 (Washington, D.C.: May 15, 2008); *DOD Business Systems Modernization: Progress Continues to Be Made in Establishing Corporate Management Controls, but Further Steps Are Needed,* GAO-07-733 (Washington, D.C.: May 14, 2007); *Business Systems Modernization: DOD Continues to Improve Institutional Approach, but Further Steps Needed,* GAO-06-658 (Washington, D.C.: May 15, 2006); and *DOD Business Systems Modernization: Important Progress Made in Establishing Foundational Architecture Products and Investment Management Practices, but Much Work Remains,* GAO-06-219 (Washington, D.C.: Nov. 23, 2005).

In May 2009, we reported that the pace of DOD's efforts in defining and implementing key institutional modernization management controls had slowed compared with progress made in each of the previous 4 years, leaving much to be accomplished to fully implement the act's requirements and related guidance.[22] In addition, between 2009 and 2011, we found that long-standing challenges we previously identified remained to be addressed.[23] For example:

- The corporate BEA had yet to be extended (i.e., federated) to the entire family of business mission area architectures, and the military departments had yet to address key enterprise architecture management practices and develop important content.

- Budget submissions included some, but omitted other, key information about business system investments, in part because of the lack of a reliable, comprehensive inventory of all defense business systems.

- The business system information used to support the development of the transition plan and DOD's budget requests, as well as certification and annual reviews, was of questionable reliability.

- DOD and the military departments had not fully defined key practices (i.e., policies and procedures) related to effectively performing both project-level (Stage 2) and portfolio-based (Stage 3) investment management as called for in the ITIM.

- Business system modernizations costing more than $1 million continued to be certified and approved, but these decisions were not always based on complete information.[24] Further, we concluded that certification and approval decisions may not be sufficiently justified because investments were certified and approved without conditions even though our prior reports had identified program weaknesses that were unresolved at the time of certification and approval.

---

[22]GAO-09-586.

[23]GAO-11-684, GAO-10-663, and GAO-09-586.

[24]Prior to the enactment of the NDAA for Fiscal Year 2012, the act required that DOD certify and approve business system modernizations greater than $1 million. As discussed subsequently in this report, the NDAA for Fiscal Year 2012 expanded this certification and approval requirement.

Accordingly, we reiterated existing recommendations and made additional recommendations to address each of these areas. DOD partially agreed with our recommendations and described actions being planned or under way to address them. Nonetheless, DOD's business systems modernization efforts remain on our high-risk list due in part to issues such as those described above.

Furthermore, in 2011, we reported[25] that none of the military department enterprise architecture programs had fully satisfied the requirements of our Enterprise Architecture Management Maturity Framework[26] and recommended that they each develop a plan to do so. Our recommendation further stated that if any department did not plan to address any element of our framework, that department should include a rationale for determining why the element was not applicable. DOD and Army concurred, and Air Force and DON did not. In this regard, DOD stated that Air Force and DON did not have a valid business case that would justify the implementation of all of our framework elements. However, Air Force and DON did not address why the elements called for by our recommendation should not be developed. Further, Army officials stated that the department had not yet issued a plan. To date, none of the military departments have addressed our recommendation.

Our most recent high-risk report noted that while DOD's capability and performance relative to business systems modernization had improved, significant challenges remained.[27] For example, the department had not fully defined and established a family of management controls, such as corporate and component business architectures and business system

---

[25]GAO, *Organizational Transformation: Military Departments Can Improve Their Enterprise Architecture Programs*, GAO-11-902 (Washington, D.C.: Sept. 26, 2011).

[26]In February 2002 and April 2003, we issued versions 1.0 and 1.1 of our Enterprise Architecture Management Maturity Framework; in August 2010, we issued a major revision (version 2.0). The framework provides a standard yet flexible benchmark against which to determine where the enterprise stands in its progress toward the ultimate goal: having a continuously improving enterprise architecture program that can serve as a featured decision support tool when considering and planning large-scale organizational restructuring or transformation initiatives. See GAO, *Organizational Transformation: A Framework for Assessing and Improving Enterprise Architecture Management (Version 2.0)*, GAO-10-846G (Washington, D.C.: August 2010); GAO-04-394G; *Information Technology: A Framework for Assessing and Improving Enterprise Architecture Management (Version 1.1)*, GAO-03-584G (Washington, D.C.: April 2003).

[27]GAO-11-278.

management processes. These management controls are vital to ensuring that DOD can effectively and efficiently manage an undertaking with the size, complexity, and significance of its business systems modernization, and minimize the associated risks.

DOD Lacks Governance Mechanisms for Institutionalizing Modernization Management Controls

DOD continues to take steps to comply with the provisions of the Ronald W. Reagan NDAA for Fiscal Year 2005, as amended, and to satisfy relevant system modernization management guidance. However, despite undertaking activities to address NDAA requirements and its future vision; the department has yet to demonstrate significant results. Specifically, DOD

- has updated its BEA and is beginning to modernize its corporate business processes, but the architecture is still not federated through development of aligned subordinate architectures for each of the military departments, and it still does not include common definitions for key terms and concepts to help ensure that the respective portions of the architecture will be properly linked and aligned.

- has not included all business system investments in its fiscal year 2013 budget submission, due in part to an unreliable inventory of all defense business systems.

- has made limited progress regarding investment management policies and procedures and has not yet established the new organizational structure and guidance that DOD has reported will address statutory requirements. In addition, while DOD implemented a business process reengineering (BPR) review process, the department is not measuring and reporting its results.

- continues to describe certification actions for its business system investments based on limited information.

- has fewer staff than it identified as needed to execute its responsibilities for business systems modernization. Specifically, the office of the DCMO, which took over these responsibilities from another office that was disestablished in 2011, reported that it had filled only 82 of its planned 139 positions, with 57 positions vacant.

DOD's limited progress in developing and implementing its federated BEA, investment management policies and procedures, and our related recommendations is due in part, to the roles and responsibilities of key organizations and senior leadership positions being largely undefined. Furthermore, the impact of DOD's efforts to reengineer its end-to-end business processes has yet to be measured and reported, and efforts to execute needed activities are limited by challenges in staffing the office of the DCMO. Until the long-standing institutional modernization management controls provided for under the act, addressed in our recommendations, and otherwise called for in best practices are fully implemented, it is likely that the department's business systems modernization will continue to be a high-risk program.

DOD Has Made Progress in Developing Its BEA but Has Not Developed Important Architecture Content or Fully Defined Roles and Responsibilities

Among other things, the act requires DOD to develop a BEA that would cover all defense business systems and their related functions and activities and that would enable the entire department to (1) comply with all federal accounting, financial management, and reporting requirements and (2) routinely produce timely, accurate, and reliable financial information for management purposes. The BEA should also include policies, procedures, data standards, and system interface requirements that are to be applied throughout the department. In addition, the NDAA for Fiscal Year 2012 added requirements that the BEA include, among other things, performance measures that are to apply uniformly throughout the department and a target defense business systems computing environment for each of DOD's major business processes. Furthermore, the act requires a BEA that extends to (i.e., federates) all defense organizational components and requires that each military department develop a well-defined enterprisewide business architecture and transition plan.

According to DOD, achieving its vision for a federated business environment requires, among other things, creating an overarching taxonomy and associated ontologies[28] that can effectively map the complex interactions and interdependencies of the department's business environment. Such a taxonomy and ontologies will provide the various components of the federated BEA with the structure and common vocabularies to help ensure that their respective portions of the architecture will be properly aligned and coordinated. In April 2011, DOD provided additional guidance that calls for the use of ontologies for

---

[28]An ontology refers to a common approach or vocabulary for how to model objects and concepts within a defined area of interest.

federating the BEA and asserting systems compliance. In addition, DOD guidance states that, because of the interrelationship among models and across architecture efforts, it is useful to define an overarching taxonomy with common definitions for key terms and concepts in the development of the architecture. The need for such a taxonomy and associated ontologies was derived from lessons learned from federation pilots conducted within the department that showed that federation of architectures was made much more difficult because of the use of different definitions to represent the same architectural data.

In addition, we have previously reported that defining and documenting roles and responsibilities is critical to the success of enterprise architecture efforts. More specifically, our Enterprise Architecture Management Maturity Framework calls for a corporate policy that identifies the major players associated with enterprise architecture development, maintenance, and use and provides for a performance and accountability framework that identifies each player's roles, responsibilities, and relationships and describes the results and outcomes for which each player is responsible and accountable.

In 2009, we reported that the then-current version of the BEA (version 6.0) addressed, to varying degrees, missing elements, inconsistencies, and usability issues that we previously identified, but that gaps still remained. In March 2012, DOD released BEA version 9.0, which continues to address the act's requirements. For example, version 9.0

- organizes BEA content around its end-to-end business processes and adds additional content associated with these processes. For example, version 9.0 added the "Accept Purchase Request" subprocess and placed this subprocess in the context of its Procure-to-Pay end-to-end business process. In addition, the Hire-to-Retire end-to-end business process includes the subprocess "Manage Benefits," which is linked to over 1,200 laws, regulations, and policies, as well as 11 subordinate business activities, such as "Manage Retirement Benefits." As a result, users can navigate the BEA to identify relevant subprocesses for each end-to-end business process and determine important laws, regulations, and policies, business capabilities, and business rules associated with a given business process.

- includes enterprise data standards for the Procure-to-Pay and Hire-to-Retire end-to-end business processes. Specifically, as part of the Procure-to-Pay end-to-end business process, enterprise standards for

Procurement Data and Purchase Request Data were added. In addition, for the Hire-to-Retire end-to-end business process, DOD updated the Common Human Resources Information Standards, which is a standard for representing common human resources management data concepts and requirements within the defense business environment. As a result, stakeholders can accelerate coordination and implementation of the high priority end-to-end business processes and related statutory requirements.

- uses a standardized business process modeling approach to represent BEA process models. For example, the BEA uses the business process modeling notation[29] standard to create a graphical representation of the "Accept Goods and Services" business process. Using a modeling approach assists DOD in its effort to eventually support automated queries of architecture information, including business models and authoritative data, to verify investment compliance and validate system solutions.

- includes performance measures and milestones for initiatives in DOD's Strategic Management Plan and relates the end-to-end business processes and operational activities documented in the BEA with the plan's initiatives and performance measures. For example, the BEA identifies that the Procure-to-Pay end-to-end business process is related to the Strategic Management Plan's measure to determine the percentage of contract obligations competitively awarded. This is important for meeting the act's new requirements associated with performance measures and to enable traceability of BEA content to the Strategic Management Plan.

DOD has defined a federated approach to its BEA that is to provide overarching governance across all business systems, functions, and activities within the DOD. This approach involves the use of semantic web technologies to provide visibility across its respective business architecture efforts. Specifically, this approach calls for the use of non-proprietary, open standards and protocols to develop DOD architectures to allow users to, among other things, locate and analyze needed architecture information across the department. Among other things, DOD's approach calls for the corporate BEA, each end-to-end business process area (e.g., Procure-to-Pay), and each DOD organization (e.g.,

---

[29]Business Process Modeling Notation is a standard for business process modeling.

Army) to establish a common vocabulary and for the programs and initiatives associated with these areas to use this vocabulary when developing their respective system and architecture products.

However, in 2011, we reported that each of the military departments had taken steps to develop architectural content, but that none had well-defined architectures to guide and constrain its business transformation initiatives.[30] Further, since May 2011, the BEA has yet to be federated through development of aligned subordinate architectures for each of the military departments. Specifically, DON reported that it has not made any significant changes to its BEA content. Army reported that it has adopted the end-to-end processes as the basis of the Army BEA, and Air Force reported that it has added additional architecture business process content and mapped some of this content to the end-to-end processes. However, each has yet to fully satisfy the requirements of our Enterprise Architecture Management Maturity Framework.[31]

In addition, the BEA does not include other important content that will be needed for achieving the office of the DCMO's vision for BEA federation. For example,

- While DOD has begun to develop a taxonomy that provides a hierarchical structure for classifying BEA information into categories, it has yet to develop an overarching taxonomy that identifies and describes all of the major terms and concepts for the business mission area. Further, version 9.0 does not include a systematic mechanism for evaluating and adding new taxonomy terms and rules for addressing ambiguous terms and descriptions. This is important since federation relies heavily on the use of taxonomy to provide the structure to link and align enterprise architectures across the business mission area, thus enabling architecture federation. Without an overarching taxonomy, there is an increased risk of not finding the most relevant content, thereby making the BEA less useful for making informed decisions regarding portfolio management and implementation of business systems solutions.

[30]GAO-11-684.

[31]GAO-11-902 and GAO-10-846G.

- DOD has begun to define corporate BEA ontologies and is developing ontologies in the human resources management area and for the U.S. Transportation Command. However, BEA 9.0 does not include ontologies for all business mission domains and organizations. According to DOD officials, each domain and organization will develop its own ontology. This is important since ontologies promote a comprehensive understanding of data and their relationships. In addition, they enable DOD to implement automated queries of information and integrate information across the department. However, DOD has yet to describe how military departments will be held accountable for executing tasks needed to be accomplished for establishing domain ontologies for their respective BEAs or whether these ontologies are also to be used for their respective corporate enterprise architecture efforts. Without these ontologies, there is an increased risk of not fully addressing the act's requirements relating to integrating budget, accounting, and program information and systems and achieving DOD's vision for a federated architecture.

DOD officials acknowledged these issues and stated that future versions of the BEA will leverage semantic technologies to create and document a common vocabulary and associated ontology. However, the department has yet to describe how each of the relevant entities will work together in developing the needed taxonomy and ontology.

In addition to describing certain content required to be in the BEA, as described earlier, the act assigns responsibility for developing portions of the BEA to various entities. The department has developed strategies that begin to document certain responsibilities associated with architecture federation. For example, the Global Information Grid Architecture Federation Strategy states that the DOD enterprise is responsible for establishing a governance structure for DOD architecture federation. The strategy also states that each mission area, such as the business mission area, is to develop and maintain mission area architectures, such as the BEA. However, given the many entities involved in BEA and DOD architecture federation, officials from the office of the DCMO have expressed concerns over who is accountable for achieving specific federation tasks and activities and how the new vision for BEA federation will be enforced.

Although our framework[32] describes the importance of having a corporate policy to govern enterprise architecture development, maintenance, and use, DOD has not developed such a policy that fully defines the roles, responsibilities, and relationships associated with developing and implementing the BEA in accordance with the act's requirements and describes the results and outcomes for which each entity involved is responsible and accountable. Without such a policy, DOD risks not moving forward with its vision for a federated BEA without having first ensured that the various entities can be held accountable for taking actions needed to ensure that the BEA will function as envisioned. Not doing so will limit the department's efforts to fully address the act's requirements and effectively use the BEA as a mechanism to achieve a streamlined and modernized defense business systems environment.

Fiscal Year 2013 Budget Submission Did Not Include Key Information on All Business Systems

Another requirement of the NDAA for Fiscal Year 2005, as amended, is that DOD's annual IT budget submission must include key information on each business system for which funding is being requested, such as the system's precertification authority and designated senior official, the appropriation type and amount of funds associated with modernization and current services (i.e., operation and maintenance), and the associated Defense Business Systems Management Committee approval decisions.

The department's fiscal year 2013 budget submission includes a range of information for 1,657[33] business system investments,[34] including the

---

[32]GAO-10-846G.

[33]Of the approximately 2,464 unique and unclassified investments in DOD's Select and Native Programming Data Input System—Information Technology (SNAP-IT), 807 are categorized as either national security systems (i.e., intelligence systems, cryptologic activities related to national security, military command and control systems, and equipment that is an integral part of a weapon or weapons system or is critical to the direct fulfillment of military or intelligence missions or systems that store, process, or communicate classified information) or are not within the business mission area (e.g., warfighting mission area).

[34]DOD's budget submission includes funding totals for past, current, and future years. Of the 1,657 business system investments included in the fiscal year 2013 budget submission, 1,394 have requested funding for fiscal year 2013. Of these systems, 205 systems have requested funding for development modernization. The remaining systems have requested funding for current services (i.e., operations and maintenance). A given system could have funding for current services as well as development modernization.

system's name, approval authority, and appropriation type.[35] The submission also identifies the amount of the fiscal year 2013 request that is for development and modernization versus operations and maintenance and notes the certification status (e.g., approved, approved with conditions, not applicable, and withdrawn) and the Defense Business Systems Management Committee approval date, where applicable.

However, similar to prior budget submissions, the fiscal year 2013 budget submission does not reflect all business system investments. To prepare the submission, DOD relied on business system investment information (e.g., funds requested, mission area, and system description) that the components entered into the department's system used to prepare its budget submission (SNAP-IT). In accordance with DOD guidance and according to DOD CIO officials, the business systems listed in SNAP-IT should match the systems listed in the Defense Information Technology Portfolio Repository (DITPR)—the department's authoritative business systems inventory. However, the DITPR data provided by DOD in March 2012 included 2,179 business systems. Therefore, SNAP-IT did not reflect about 500 business systems that were identified in DITPR.[36]

In 2009, we reported that the information between SNAP-IT and DITPR data repositories were not consistent and, accordingly, recommended that DOD develop and implement plans for reconciling and validating the completeness and reliability of information in its two repositories, and to include information on the status of these efforts in the department's fiscal year 2010 report in response to the act.[37] DOD agreed with the need to

---

[35]According to the DOD CIO official responsible for the SNAP-IT system, this report reflects information contained in SNAP-IT as of January 2012. The NDAA for Fiscal Year 2012 (10 U.S.C. § 2222(h)(3)) calls for the submission to identify both the system's pre-certification authority and the senior official for the functions and activities supported by the defense business system under review. However, prior to the NDAA for Fiscal Year 2012, the requirement was that the approval authority be identified. The NDAA for Fiscal Year 2012 was signed into law on December 31, 2011, which according to DOD, did not provide sufficient time to update the SNAP-IT data to reflect the act's new requirements. The official responsible for the SNAP-IT system stated that the fiscal year 2014 budget request would be updated to reflect the requirements of the act, as amended.

[36]The difference between the number of systems reported in DITPR and SNAP-IT is about 500 because the 1,657 business systems listed in SNAP-IT includes some systems that are not listed in the DITPR data DOD provided to us. DITPR also includes systems that are not listed in SNAP-IT.

[37]GAO-09-586.

reconcile information between the two repositories and stated that it had begun to take actions to address this. In 2011, we reported that, according to the office of the DOD CIO, efforts to provide automated SNAP-IT and DITPR integration work were delayed due to increased SNAP-IT requirements in supporting the fiscal year 2012 budget submission and ongoing reorganization efforts within the department. DOD officials also told us that the department planned to restart the process of integrating the two repositories beginning in the third quarter of fiscal year 2011.[38]

Since that time, DOD CIO officials have reiterated the department's commitment to integrating the two repositories and taken steps toward achieving this end. For example, the officials stated that they have added a field to the DITPR repository that allows components to identify an individual system as a defense business system. These officials added that this change, once fully implemented, will be a key to providing automated DITPR and SNAP-IT integration. The Deputy DOD CIO (Resources) has also sent memoranda to specific DOD components identifying systems listed in DITPR that are not properly associated with systems identified in SNAP-IT and requesting that the components take action to address these inconsistencies. Nevertheless, DOD CIO officials responsible for the DITPR and SNAP-IT repositories stated that efforts to integrate them continue to be limited by ongoing organizational changes and the time required to address new system requirements unrelated to integrating the repositories. For example, these officials cited slowdowns resulting from the recent disestablishment of DOD's Networks and Information Integration organization, as well as time spent making adjustments to the SNAP-IT repository to accommodate new Office of Management and Budget reporting requirements.[39] They added that all data are owned by the components and therefore it is ultimately the responsibility of the components to update their respective data. However, DOD has not established a deadline by which it intends to complete the integration of the repositories and validate the completeness and reliability of information.

---

[38]GAO-11-684.

[39]According to DOD CIO officials, these changes were associated with changes in Office of Management and Budget Circular A-11 reporting requirements.

Until DOD has a reliable, comprehensive inventory of all defense business systems, it will not be able to ensure the completeness and reliability of the department's IT budget submissions. Moreover, the lack of current and accurate information increases the risk of oversight decisions that are not prudent and justified.

DOD Has Not Yet Redefined Its Investment Management Process

DOD has made limited progress in defining and implementing investment management policies and procedures as required by the act and addressed in our ITIM framework since our last review in 2011. In addition, while the department has reported its intent to implement a new organizational structure and guidance to address statutory requirements, this structure and guidance have yet to be established. DOD also continues to approve investments on the basis of BEA compliance assessments that have not been validated. Further, while DOD has conducted various BPR activities related to its business system investments and underlying business processes, the department has not yet begun to measure associated results. Thus, the extent to which these efforts have streamlined and improved the efficiency of the underlying business processes remains uncertain.

DOD Is Working to Improve Business System Investment Management, but Progress Is Slow

The act requires DOD to establish an IRB and investment management processes that are consistent with the investment management provisions of the Clinger-Cohen Act of 1996.[40] As we have previously reported, organizations that satisfy Stages 2 and 3 of our ITIM framework[41] have the investment selection, control, and evaluation governance structures, and the related policies, procedures, and practices that are consistent with the investment management provisions

---

[40]See 40 U.S.C. § 11312.

[41]GAO-04-394G. Our ITIM framework consists of five progressive stages of maturity for any given agency relative to selecting, controlling, and evaluating its investment management capabilities. Stage 2 includes five critical processes and nine related key practices that call for policies and procedures associated with effective project-level investment management. Stage 3 includes four critical processes and five related key practices that call for policies and procedures associated with effective portfolio-based investment management.

of the Clinger-Cohen Act. We have used the framework in many of our evaluations, and a number of agencies have adopted it.[42]

In 2011, we reported that DOD had continued to establish investment management processes described in our ITIM framework but had not fully defined all key practices. For example, we reported that DOD had fully implemented two critical processes associated with capturing investment information and meeting business needs, and partially completed the Stage 2 critical process associated with instituting an investment board. However, the department had yet to address other critical processes, including those associated with selecting investments and providing investment oversight.

Since 2011, DOD has not fully implemented any additional key practices.[43] Furthermore, the military departments have made very little progress in addressing elements of our ITIM framework that we previously reported as unsatisfied. For example,

- In 2011, we reported that Air Force had implemented four key practices related to effectively managing investments as individual business system programs (Stage 2). The Air Force had also addressed a key practice associated with portfolio-level investment management (Stage 3) — assigning responsibility for the development and modification of IT portfolio selection criteria. However, it has not implemented any additional practices since that time. The Air Force has described its intent to change its IT investment management structure and form a new branch to lay the foundation for integrated, efficient IT portfolio management processes; however, according to Air Force officials, this office is not yet fully established and faces competing personnel issues within the department. Further, Air Force officials stated that they are working to update the department's IT portfolio management and IT investment guidance, but the updates are not expected to be issued until November 2012.

---

[42]See, for example, GAO, *Information Technology: HUD Needs to Better Define Commitments and Disclose Risks for Modernization Projects in Future Expenditure Plans*, GAO-11-72 (Washington, D.C.: Nov. 23, 2010).

[43]GAO-11-684.

- In 2011, we reported that DON had implemented four key practices related to effectively managing investments as individual business system programs (Stage 2) and one key practice related to managing IT investments as a portfolio of programs (Stage 3). Since that time, DON has not fully implemented any additional key practices. While the department demonstrated that it has documented policies and procedures related to establishing assessment standards to describe a program's health (e.g., cost, schedule, and performance), these policies and procedures do not describe the enterprisewide IT investment board's role in reviewing and making decisions based on this information. Such a description is important because the investment board has ultimate responsibility for making decisions about IT investments.

- In 2011, we reported that Army had implemented two key practices associated with capturing investment information. Specifically, it had established policies and procedures for collecting information about the department's investments and had assigned responsibility for investment information collection and accuracy. These are activities associated with effectively managing investments as individual business system programs (Stage 2). However, with regard to managing IT investments as a portfolio of programs (Stage 3), the Army had not fully defined any of the five key practices. Further, since that time, the Army has not fully implemented any additional Stage 2 or Stage 3 practices. Army officials stated that the department has been focused on performing extensive portfolio reviews that are intended to inform many of the ITIM key practices and lead to updates of its investment management policies and procedures. As of April 2012, Army officials stated that the department had completed its first round of portfolio reviews. According to Army officials, the department has also worked to release its Business Systems Information Technology Implementation Plan, which is to provide details for its investment management strategy, due as part of the 2012 Army Campaign Plan; however, this plan has not yet been released.

According to the department, the slow progress made on the investment management process at DOD and the military departments in the past year is due, in part, to the department's activities to address the new

NDAA for Fiscal Year 2012 requirements.[44] Specifically, in April 2012, DOD reported that it was in the process of constituting a single IRB.[45] According to DOD, this IRB is to replace the existing governance structure and is to be operational by October 2012. In addition, DOD reported that it intends to incrementally implement an expanded investment review process that analyzes business system investments using common decision criteria and establishes investment priorities while ensuring integration with the department's budgeting process. The department has stated its intention to use our ITIM model to assess its ability to comply with its related investment selection and control requirements. Further, DOD officials stated that this new investment review process will encompass a portfolio-based approach to investment management that is to employ a structured methodology for classifying and assessing business investments in useful views across the department. DOD officials stated that an initial review of all systems requiring certification under the new NDAA requirements is also planned to be completed by the start of the new fiscal year.

While the department has reported its intent to implement this new organizational structure and guidance to address statutory requirements and redefine the process by which the department selects, evaluates, and controls business systems investments, this structure and guidance have yet to be established. DOD officials stated that the process has not yet been completed because they want to make sure they consider the best approach for investment management going forward. Accordingly, DOD is taking a phased approach as described in the department's congressional report, which it intends to fully implement by October 2012.

---

[44]The NDAA for Fiscal Year 2012 requires DOD to certify and approve covered defense business programs that have a total cost in excess of $1 million over the period of the current Future-Years Defense Program, which is the department's financial plan over a 6-year period. The act also provides DOD with flexibility in establishing an IRB structure to oversee these investments, but requires DOD to establish an IRB and investment management process, consistent with the act, to review and certify the planning, design, acquisition, development, deployment, operation, maintenance, modernization, and project costs, benefits, and risks of covered defense business systems programs by March 15, 2012.

[45]DOD, *Department of Defense Investment Review Board and Investment Management Process for Defense Business Systems: Report to Congress March 2012 Pursuant to Section 901 of the National Defense Authorization Act for Fiscal Year 2012*. According to DOD, this report responds to the new 10 U.S.C. § 2222 requirements for DOD to define and establish an IRB and investment management process by March 15, 2012.

While it is too soon to evaluate the department's updated approach to business system investment management, we will further evaluate DOD's progress in defining and implementing its updated investment review processes in our fiscal year 2013 report on defense business systems modernization. Until DOD redefines and implements its investment management processes by the established deadline and until the military departments make additional progress on their own investment management processes, it is unlikely that the thousands of DOD business system investments will be managed in a consistent, repeatable, and effective manner.

DOD Continues to Certify and Approve Investments Based on Limited Information

Since 2005, DOD has been required to certify and approve all business system modernizations costing more than $1 million[46] to ensure that they meet specific conditions defined in the act. This process includes asserting that an investment is compliant with the BEA.

The department continues to approve investments on the basis of architecture compliance. However, the department's policy and guidance associated with architecture compliance still does not call for compliance assertions to be validated and officials agreed that not all of the compliance information has been validated. Department officials stated that some information associated with the compliance process has been validated, such as information associated with complying with DOD's Standard Financial Information Structure.[47] In 2008, we made recommendations that the department amend existing policy and requirements to explicitly call for such validation to occur.[48] DOD agreed with our findings and recommendations and stated that it planned to assign validation responsibilities and issue guidance that described the methodology for performing validation activities. Nonetheless, the department has not yet addressed our recommendation.

---

[46]The obligation of DOD funds for a covered defense business system program that has not been certified and approved in accordance with subsection (a) is a violation of 10 U.S.C. § 1341(a)(1)(A).

[47]The Standard Financial Information Structure is intended to provide a standard financial management data structure and uniformity throughout DOD in reporting on the results of operations.

[48]GAO, *DOD Business Systems Modernization: Key Navy Programs' Compliance with DOD's Federated Business Enterprise Architecture Needs to Be Adequately Demonstrated*, GAO-08-972 (Washington, D.C.: Aug. 7, 2008).

Among other things, BEA compliance is important for helping to ensure that DOD programs have been optimized to support DOD operations. However, as we have reported, without proper validation of compliance assertions, there is an increased risk that DOD will make business system investment decisions based on information that is inaccurate and unreliable. Under DOD's vision for a semantic BEA, described previously in this report, officials have stated that compliance validations will be conducted automatically using specialized software tools as program architecture artifacts are developed. However, until DOD achieves its semantic BEA vision and addresses our prior recommendation, compliance assertions will continue to be unvalidated.

DOD Has Begun Performing Required BPR Assessments, but the Results of These Efforts Are Not Yet Being Measured

In addition to the requirement that covered business systems be certified and approved to be in compliance with the BEA, the act requires that the Chief Management Officer certify that these business systems have undergone appropriate BPR activities.[49] BPR is an approach for redesigning the way work is performed to better support an organization's mission and reduce costs. After considering an organization's mission, strategic goals, and customer needs, reengineering focuses on improving an organization's business processes. We have issued BPR guidance that, among other things, discusses the importance of having meaningful performance measures to assess whether BPR activities actually achieve the intended results.[50] In this regard, the act, as amended, identifies intended results of BPR reviews such as ensuring that the business process to be supported by the defense business system will be as streamlined and efficient as practicable and the need to tailor commercial-off-the-shelf systems to meet unique requirements or incorporate unique

---

[49]For nonmilitary department programs and programs supporting business processes of more than one military department or defense agency, the DCMO is responsible for making a determination that sufficient BPR was conducted. For military department programs, the Chief Management Officer of the respective department is responsible for making a determination that sufficient BPR was conducted.

[50]GAO, *Business Process Reengineering Assessment Guide (Version 3)*, GAO/AIMD-10.1.15, (Washington, D.C.: May 1997).

interfaces has been eliminated or reduced to the maximum extent practicable.[51]

While DOD has conducted various BPR activities, including preparing BPR assessment guidance; conducting assessments to meet the act's requirements; and performing other BPR efforts including refining its end-to-end business processes, the department has not yet begun to measure associated results. The department's BPR activities are summarized as follows:

- DOD issued interim guidance in April 2010 and final guidance in April 2011 to assist programs in addressing the act's BPR requirement.[52] This guidance describes the types of documentation required for systems seeking certification, including a standardized BPR assessment form, and illustrates the process for submitting documentation for review and approval. DOD's final BPR guidance related to system certification generally comports with key practices described in our guidance. For example, DOD's guidance recognizes the importance of developing a clear problem statement and business case, analyzing the as-is and to-be environments, and developing a change management approach for implementing the new business process.

- Consistent with its guidance, DOD has begun to implement its BPR review process in an effort to meet the act's requirements. Specifically, all systems in fiscal year 2011 submitted BPR assessment forms for review. In addition, the DCMO and military department Chief Management Officers are in the process of signing formal determinations that sufficient BPR was conducted with respect to each program.

- The department has also performed BPR to respond to specific needs that have been identified by departmental components and to refine its end-to-end business processes. For example, the Defense

---

[51]This requirement was first added by the NDAA for fiscal year 2010. The act's requirements for systems certified and approved during fiscal year 2011 only applied to business system modernizations greater than $1 million. The NDAA for fiscal year 2012 applies this requirement to all business systems expecting to spend a total of $1 million over the course of the Future-Years Defense Program.

[52]DOD Deputy Chief Management Officer, *Guidance for the Implementation of Section 1072 – Business Process Reengineering*, April 30, 2011.

Commissary Agency, in cooperation with the Business Transformation Agency and now the office of the DCMO, used BPR to help formulate a future enterprise transition plan for the agency. In addition, DOD officials described activities to refine DOD's debt management business process, which is part of the Budget-to-Report end-to-end process. The standardization of related business process models related to debt management led to updates in the latest BEA, which now provide tools that can be used to guide and constrain investments.

While DOD has performed the BPR activities described above, the extent to which these efforts have streamlined and improved the efficiency of the underlying business processes remains uncertain because the department has yet to establish specific measures and report outcomes that align with the department's efforts. For example, the department does not track information, such as the number of systems that have undergone material process changes or the number of interfaces reduced or eliminated as a result of BPR reviews. DOD officials noted that addressing these requirements has been challenging and measuring progress, such as the number of interfaces reduced, has not been a priority. However, until the department develops and reports on performance measures associated with the development of its end-to-end processes and their related BPR activities, the department and its stakeholders will not know the extent to which BPR is effectively streamlining and improving its end-to-end business processes as intended.

DOD's Annual Report Continues to Describe Certification Actions for Its Business System Investments

Among other things, the act requires DOD to include, in its annual report to congressional defense committees, a description of specific actions the department has taken on each business system submitted for certification.[53] As applicable in fiscal year 2011, the act required that modernization investments involving more than $1 million in obligations be certified by a designated approval authority[54] as meeting specific

---

[53]10 U.S.C. § 2222 (i)(1)(B).

[54]For fiscal year 2011, the approval authorities include the Under Secretary of Defense for Acquisition, Technology, and Logistics; the Under Secretary of Defense (Comptroller); the Under Secretary of Defense for Personnel and Readiness; DOD CIO; and the Deputy Secretary of Defense. They are responsible for the review, approval, and oversight of business systems and must establish investment review processes for systems under their cognizance.

criteria, such as whether or not the system is in compliance with DOD's BEA and appropriate BPR efforts have been undertaken. Further, the act requires that the Defense Business Systems Management Committee approve each of these certifications.

DOD's annual report identifies that the Defense Business Systems Management Committee approved 198 actions to certify, decertify, or recertify defense business system modernizations.[55] These 198 IRB certification actions represented a total of about $2.2 billion in modernization spending. Specifically, the annual report states that during fiscal year 2011, the Defense Business Systems Management Committee approved 58 unique certifications, 102 recertifications, and 38 decertifications—101 with and 97 without conditions. Examples of conditions associated with individual systems include conditions related to business process engineering[56] and BEA compliance.[57]

While DOD has continued to report its certification actions, these actions have been based on limited information, such as unvalidated architecture compliance assertions, as discussed in the previous section. Until DOD addresses our prior recommendations, the department faces increased risk that it will not effectively be able to oversee its extensive business systems investments.

DCMO Lacks Staff It Identified as Needed to Support Departmentwide Business Systems Modernization

Among other things, the act calls for the DCMO to be responsible and accountable for developing and maintaining the BEA, as well as integrating defense business operations. Although responsibility for these activities previously resided with the Business Transformation Agency, DOD announced the disestablishment of this agency in August 2010. In June 2011, we recommended that DOD expeditiously complete the implementation of the announced transfer of functions of the agency and provide specificity as to when and where these functions will be

---

[55]An individual system can have multiple certification actions during a single fiscal year.

[56]For example, a condition levied on the Navy Future Personnel and Pay Solution System called for the program to provide improved Business Problem statements with appropriate measures. This condition was marked as satisfied on November 30, 2011.

[57]For example, a condition levied on the Global Combat Support System—Army calls for the submission of an updated BEA compliance checklist. The condition was marked closed on August 26, 2011.

transferred.[58] Subsequently, the DCMO defined an organizational structure consisting of a front office and six directorates and identified the staff resources it would need to fulfill its new responsibilities, which became effective in September 2011.

However, the office reported that it has not yet filled many of the positions needed to execute these responsibilities. In particular, as of April 2012, the office reported that it had filled only 82 of its planned 139 positions, with 57 positions (41 percent) remaining unfilled.[59] For example, the office had filled only 12 of 43 positions within its Technology, Innovation, and Engineering Directorate; which, among other things, is responsible for developing the BEA. Further, only 10 of 19 positions within the Planning and Performance Management Directorate, 14 of 22 positions within its Business Integration Directorate, and 16 of 23 positions within its Investment and Acquisition Management Directorate had been filled. Table 3 identifies the key responsibilities of each DCMO organizational component as well as planned and actual staffing.

Table 3: DCMO Organizational Components, Key Responsibilities, and Planned and Actual Staffing

Organizational component	Key responsibilities	Planned staff	Actual staff
Front Office	Provide executive leadership and staff support.	9	7
Investment and Acquisition Management Directorate	Provide acquisition oversight. Operate and maintain the IRB(s). Lead IT acquisition reform, including implementation of the Business Capability Lifecycle.	23	16
Business Integration Directorate	Reengineer and apply end-to-end processes to improve business operations and support audit readiness. Manage and oversee the appropriate end-to-end governance model(s) and forum(s).	22	14
Technology, Innovation, and Engineering Directorate	Build and deliver the BEA. Lead DOD in engineering advanced technical standards to support BEA federation.	43	12

[58]GAO-11-684.

[59]These numbers do not count as filled 12 positions that the office of the DCMO reported it had selected individuals to fill, but for which those individuals have not yet officially reported.

Organizational component	Key responsibilities	Planned staff	Actual staff
Planning and Performance Management Directorate	Develop the Strategic Management Plan and enterprise transition plan.	19	10
	Report to Congress on progress and improvements made in the DOD Business Mission Area.		
	Conduct and manage process improvement projects.		
	Conduct and manage process improvement and BPR training.		
Expeditionary Business Operations Directorate	Provide subject matter expertise on deployed end-to-end business operations and deploy system architecture development/optimization.	11	11
Operations Directorate	Manage the day-to-day operations of the office of the DCMO (e.g., human resources, budgeting, IT).	12	12
Total		**139**	**82**

Source: GAO based on DOD documentation.

Note: This table reflects planned and actual government staff positions. It does not include contractor positions.

Key leadership positions were among those that were unfilled. Specifically, according to officials from the office of the DCMO, the positions for the Directors of the Business Integration and the Technology, Innovation, and Engineering Directorates had not been filled as of late April 2012.[60] Moreover, the position for the Director of the Planning and Performance Management Directorate, while previously staffed, was vacant as of April 1, 2012.

Officials from the office of the DCMO attributed the office's unfilled positions to, among other things, challenges associated with the length of time between when DOD announced that the Business Transformation Agency, which previously addressed many of the DCMO's current functions, would be disestablished (August 2010) and when the agency was formally disestablished (September 2011). For example, some staff chose to seek employment elsewhere due to uncertainties associated with the transition. While DOD stated that the office is taking steps to fill the vacant positions, the lack of staff in important DCMO directorates such as those responsible for building and delivering the BEA; managing business system acquisitions; reengineering end-to-end business processes; and developing DOD's Strategic Management Plan and enterprise transition plan has caused the office to prioritize what it can and cannot do.

---

[60]The office of the DCMO reported that individuals had been identified to fill two of the three unfilled positions, but those individuals have not yet officially reported.

Conclusions

Establishing a well-defined, federated BEA and modernizing DOD's business systems and processes are critical to effectively improving the department's business systems environment. The department is taking steps to establish such a business architecture and modernize its business systems and processes, but long-standing challenges remain. Specifically, while DOD had made progress in developing its corporate enterprise architecture, it has yet to be federated through the development of aligned subordinate architectures for each of the military departments. The department has also taken effective steps to establish an infrastructure for establishing a federated BEA, including documenting a vision for the BEA and developing content around its end-to-end business processes. However, the department's ability to achieve its federated BEA vision is limited by the lack of common definitions for key terms and concepts to help ensure that each of the respective portions of the architecture will be properly linked and aligned, as well as by the absence of a policy that clarifies roles, responsibilities, and accountability mechanisms. In addition, information used to support the development of the DOD's budget requests continues to be of questionable reliability and no deadline for validating reliable information has been set. DOD has also not implemented key practices from our ITIM framework since our last review in 2011. Further, while the department has begun taking steps to reengineer its business systems and processes, and has issued sound guidance for conducting BPR associated with individual business systems, it has yet to measure and report on the impact these efforts have had on streamlining and simplifying its corporate business processes. Finally, the efforts of the office of the DCMO have been impacted by having fewer staff than the office identified as needed to support departmentwide business systems modernization.

Collectively, these limitations continue to put the billions of dollars spent annually on about 2,200 business system investments that support DOD functions, such as departmentwide financial management and military personnel health care at risk. Our previous recommendations to the department have been aimed at accomplishing these and other important activities related to its business systems modernization. While the department has agreed with these recommendations, its progress in addressing the act's requirements, its vision for a federated architecture, and our related recommendations is limited, in part, by continued uncertainty surrounding the roles and responsibilities of key organizations and senior leadership positions. In light of this, it is essential that the Secretary of Defense issue a policy that resolves these issues, as doing so is necessary for the department to establish the full range of institutional management controls needed to address its business systems modernization high-risk area. It is equally important that DOD measure the impact of its BPR efforts and include information on the results of these efforts and its efforts to fully staff the office of the DCMO in the department's annual report in response to the act.

Recommendations for Executive Action

Because we have existing recommendations that address many of the institutional management control weaknesses discussed in this report, we reiterate those recommendations.

In addition, to ensure that DOD continues to implement the full range of institutional management controls needed to address its business systems modernization high-risk area, we recommend that the Secretary of Defense ensure that the Deputy Secretary of Defense, as the department's Chief Management Officer, establish a policy that clarifies the roles, responsibilities, and relationships among the Chief Management Officer, Deputy Chief Management Officer, DOD and military department Chief Information Officers, Principal Staff Assistants, military department Chief Management Officers, and the heads of the military departments and defense agencies, associated with the development of a federated BEA. Among other things, the policy should address the development and implementation of an overarching taxonomy and associated ontologies to help ensure that each of the respective portions of the architecture will be properly linked and aligned. In addition, the policy should address alignment and coordination of business process areas, military department and defense agency activities associated with developing and implementing each of the various components of the BEA, and relationships among these entities.

To ensure that annual budget submissions are based on complete and accurate information, we recommend that the Secretary of Defense direct the appropriate DOD organizations to establish a deadline by which it intends to complete the integration of the repositories and validate the completeness and reliability of information.

To facilitate congressional oversight and promote departmental accountability, we recommend that the Secretary of Defense ensure that the Deputy Secretary of Defense, as the department's Chief Management Officer, direct the Deputy Chief Management Officer to include in DOD's annual report to Congress on compliance with 10 U.S.C. § 2222,

- the results of the department's BPR efforts. Among other things, the results should include the department's determination of the number of systems that have undergone material process changes, the number of interfaces eliminated as part of these efforts (i.e., by program, by name), and the status of its end-to-end business process reengineering efforts, and

- an update on the office of the DCMO's progress toward filling staff positions and the impact of any unfilled positions on the ability of the office to conduct its work.

Agency Comments and Our Evaluation

In written comments on a draft of this report, signed by the Deputy Chief Management Officer and reprinted in appendix II, the department partially concurred with our first recommendation, concurred with our second and third recommendations, and did not concur with the remaining recommendation.

The department partially concurred with our first recommendation to establish a policy that clarifies the roles, responsibilities, and relationships among its various management officials associated with the development of a federated BEA. In particular, the department stated its belief that officials' roles, relationships, and responsibilities are already sufficiently defined through statute, policy, and practice, and that additional guidance is not needed. However, the department added that it will continue to look for opportunities to strengthen and expand guidance, to include the new investment management and architecture processes. We do not agree that officials' roles, relationships, and responsibilities are sufficiently defined in existing policy. For example, we found that DOD has not developed a policy that fully defines the roles, responsibilities, and relationships associated with developing and implementing the BEA. Moreover, in our view, responsibility and accountability for architecture federation will not be effectively addressed with additional guidance because guidance cannot be enforced. Rather, we believe a policy, which can be enforced, will more effectively establish responsibility and accountability for architecture federation. Without a policy, the department risks not moving forward with its vision for a federated architecture. Thus, we continue to believe our recommendation is warranted.

The department concurred with our second recommendation, to establish a deadline by which it intends to complete the integration of the repositories and validate the completeness and reliability of information, and described commitments and actions being planned or under way. We support the department's efforts to address our recommendation and reiterate the importance of following through in implementing the recommendation within the stated time frame.

DOD also concurred with our third recommendation that the Deputy Secretary of Defense, as the department's Chief Management Officer, direct the Deputy Chief Management Officer to include the results of the department's BPR efforts in its annual report to Congress. However, the department stated that given the passage of the NDAA for Fiscal Year 2012, BPR authority now rests with the military department Chief Management Officers. As such, DOD stated that it would be appropriate for the recommendation to be directed to the BPR owners. We agree that the act requires the appropriate precertification authority for each covered business system to determine that appropriate BPR efforts have been undertaken. However, we disagree that our recommendation should be directed to the BPR owners. The recommendation is not intended to be prescriptive as to who should measure the impact of the BPR efforts. Rather, it calls for the reporting of the results of such efforts in the department's annual report to Congress, which is prepared by the office of the DCMO under the department's Chief Management Officer.

The department did not concur with our fourth recommendation to provide an update on the office of the DCMO's progress toward filling staff positions and the impact of any unfilled positions in its annual report to Congress. DOD stated that it does not believe that the annual report is the appropriate communication mechanism; however, it offered to provide us with an update. While we support the department's willingness to provide us with an update, we, nonetheless, stand by our recommendation. The purpose of the annual report is to document the department's progress in improving its business operations through defense business systems modernization. Thus, the potential for staffing shortfalls in the office of the DCMO to adversely impact the department's progress should be communicated to the department's congressional stakeholders as part of the report. Including information about the department's progress in staffing the office that was recently established to be responsible for business systems modernization would not only facilitate congressional oversight, but also promote departmental accountability.

We are sending copies of this report to the appropriate congressional committees; the Director, Office of Management and Budget; the Secretary of Defense; and other interested parties. This report also is available at no charge on the GAO website at http://www.gao.gov.

If you or your staff members have any questions on matters discussed in this report, please contact me at (202) 512-6304 or melvinv@gao.gov. Contact points for our Offices of Congressional Relations and Public Affairs may be found on the last page of this report. GAO staff who made major contributions to this report are listed in appendix III.

Valerie C. Melvin
Director
Information Management and Technology Resources Issues

List of Committees

The Honorable Carl Levin
Chairman
The Honorable John McCain
Ranking Member
Committee on Armed Services
United States Senate

The Honorable Daniel Inouye
Chairman
The Honorable Thad Cochran
Ranking Member
Subcommittee on Defense
Committee on Appropriations
United States Senate

The Honorable Howard P. McKeon
Chairman
The Honorable Adam Smith
Ranking Member
Committee on Armed Services
House of Representatives

The Honorable C.W. Bill Young
Chairman
The Honorable Norman Dicks
Ranking Member
Subcommittee on Defense
Committee on Appropriations
House of Representatives

Appendix I: Objective, Scope, and Methodology

As agreed with the congressional defense committees, our objective was to assess the Department of Defense's (DOD) actions to comply with key aspects of section 332 of the National Defense Authorization Act (NDAA) for Fiscal Year 2005 (the act), as amended, 10 U.S.C. § 2222[1] and related federal guidance. These include (1) developing a business enterprise architecture (BEA) and a transition plan for implementing the architecture, (2) identifying systems information in its annual budget submission, (3) establishing a system investment approval and accountability structure along with an investment review process, and (4) certifying and approving any business system program costing in excess of $1 million. (See the background section of this report for additional information on the act's requirements.) Our methodology relative to each of the four provisions is as follows:

To address the architecture, we analyzed version 9.0 of the BEA, which was released on March 15, 2012, relative to the act's specific architectural requirements and related guidance that our previous annual reports in response to the act identified as not being fully implemented.[2] Specifically, we interviewed office of the Deputy Chief Management Officer (DCMO) officials and reviewed written responses and related documentation on steps completed, under way, or planned to address these weaknesses. We then reviewed architectural artifacts in BEA 9.0 to validate the responses and identify any discrepancies. We also determined the extent to which BEA 9.0 addressed 10 U.S.C. § 2222, as amended by the NDAA for Fiscal Year 2012. In addition, we analyzed documentation and interviewed knowledgeable DOD officials about efforts to establish a federated business mission area enterprise architecture. Further, we reviewed the military departments' responses regarding actions taken or planned to address our previous recommendations on the maturity of their respective enterprise architecture programs.[3] We did not determine whether the DOD Enterprise Transition Plan addressed the requirements specified in the act, because an updated plan was not released during the time we were conducting our audit work.

---

[1]Ronald W. Reagan National Defense Authorization Act for Fiscal Year 2005, Pub. L. No. 108-375, § 332, 118 Stat. 1811, 1851-1856 (Oct. 28, 2004), as amended.

[2]See, for example, GAO-09-586 and GAO-11-684.

[3]GAO-11-902.

To determine whether DOD's fiscal year 2013 IT budget submission was
prepared in accordance with the criteria set forth in the act, we reviewed
and analyzed the Report on Defense Business System Modernization
Fiscal Year 2005 National Defense Authorization Act, Section 332, dated
March 2012, and compared it with the specific requirements in the act.
We also compared information contained in the department's system that
is used to prepare its budget submission (SNAP-IT) with information in
the department's authoritative business systems inventory (DITPR) to
determine if DOD's fiscal year 2013 budget request included all business
systems and assessed the extent to which DOD has made progress in
addressing our related recommendation. In addition, we reviewed DOD's
budget submission to determine the extent to which it addresses 10
U.S.C. § 2222, as amended by the NDAA for Fiscal Year 2012. We also
analyzed selected business system information contained in DITPR, such
as system life cycle start and end dates, to validate the reliability of the
information. We also interviewed officials from the office of DOD's Chief
Information Officer (CIO) to discuss the accuracy and
comprehensiveness of information contained in the SNAP-IT system, the
discrepancies in the information contained in the DITPR and SNAP-IT
systems, and efforts under way or planned to address these
discrepancies.

To assess the establishment of DOD enterprise and component
investment management structures and processes, we followed up on
related weaknesses that our previous reports in response to the act have
identified as not being fully implemented. Specifically, we interviewed the
office of the DCMO and military department officials and reviewed written
responses and related documentation on steps completed, under way, or
planned to address these weaknesses. We also met with cognizant
officials on steps taken to address new investment management
requirements of the NDAA for Fiscal Year 2012. Further, we reviewed
DOD's most recent BEA compliance guidance to determine the extent to
which it addressed our related open recommendations. Finally, we
reviewed business process reengineering documentation provided to
support assertions that modernization programs had undergone business
process reengineering assessments.

To determine whether the department was certifying and approving
business system investments with annual obligations exceeding $1
million, we reviewed and analyzed all Defense Business Systems
Management Committee certification approval memoranda. We also
reviewed IRB certification memoranda issued prior to the Defense
Business Systems Management Committee's final approval decisions for

fiscal year 2011. We contacted officials from the office of the DCMO and investment review boards to discuss any discrepancies. In addition, we discussed with officials from the office of the DCMO its plans for updating the investment review process consistent with requirements of the NDAA for Fiscal Year 2012 and obtained related documentation. To assess the office of the DCMO's progress toward filling staff positions, we compared the number of authorized positions with the staff on board as of late April 2012; reviewed and analyzed related staffing documentation; and interviewed office of the DCMO officials about staffing.

We did not independently validate the reliability of the cost and budget figures provided by DOD because the specific amounts were not relevant to our findings. We conducted this performance audit at DOD offices in Arlington and Alexandria, Virginia, from September 2011 to June 2012 in accordance with generally accepted government auditing standards. Those standards require that we plan and perform the audit to obtain sufficient, appropriate evidence to provide a reasonable basis for our findings and conclusions based on our audit objectives. We believe that the evidence obtained provides a reasonable basis for our findings and conclusions based on our audit objective.

Appendix II: Comments from the Department of Defense

DEPUTY CHIEF MANAGEMENT OFFICER
9010 DEFENSE PENTAGON
WASHINGTON, DC 20301-9010

MAY 23 2012

Ms. Valerie Melvin
Director, Information Management and Technology Resources Issues
U.S. Government Accountability Office
441 G Street, NW
Washington, DC 20548

Dear Ms. Melvin,

    This is the Department of Defense (DoD) response to the Government Accountability Office (GAO) draft report GAO-12-685, "DOD BUSINESS SYSTEMS MODERNIZATION: Governance Mechanisms for Implementing Management Controls Need to be Improved," dated May 14, 2012, (GAO Code 310975). The Department partially concurs with the first recommendation, concurs with the second and third recommendations, and non-concurs with the fourth recommendation contained in the draft report.

    The Department appreciates the opportunity to respond to your draft report. We look forward to your continued cooperation and dialog toward our common goal of improving business systems modernization throughout the Department of Defense. Should you have any questions please contact Mr. Bryan Kitchens, 571-371-3182, bryan.kitchens@osd.mil.

Sincerely,

Elizabeth A. McGrath

Enclosure:
As stated

GAO DRAFT REPORT DATED MAY 14, 2012
GAO-12-685 (GAO CODE 310975)

"DOD BUSINESS SYSTEMS MODERNIZATION: GOVERNANCE
MECHANISMS FOR IMPLEMENTING MANAGEMENT CONTROLS NEED
TO BE IMPROVED"

DEPARTMENT OF DEFENSE COMMENTS
TO THE GAO RECOMMENDATIONS

RECOMMENDATION 1: The GAO recommends that the Secretary of Defense ensure
that the Deputy Secretary of Defense, as the department's Chief Management Officer,
establish a policy that clarifies the roles, responsibilities, and relationships among the
Chief Management Officer, Deputy Chief Management Officer, DOD and military
department Chief Information Officers, Principle Staff Assistants, military department
Chief Management Officers, and the heads of the military departments and defense
agencies, associated with the development of a federated BEA. Among other things, the
policy should address the development and implementation of an overarching taxonomy
and associated ontologies to help ensure that each of the respective portfolios of
architecture will be properly linked and aligned. In addition, the policy should address
alignment and coordination of business process areas, military department and defense
agency activities associated with developing and implementing each of the various
components of the BEA, and relationships among these entities.

DoD RESPONSE: Partially concur.

The Department of Defense (DoD) partially concurs with the recommendation made by
the Government Accountability Office (GAO) to establish formal policy to clarify the
roles, relationships, and responsibilities of its various management officials. While the
Department believes that the roles, relationships, and responsibilities between its officials
for the business enterprise architecture and its business processes are already sufficiently
defined through statute, policy, and practice and that additional guidance is not needed,
we will continue to look for opportunities to strengthen and expand guidance, to include
our new investment management and architecture processes.

RECOMMENDATION 2: The GAO recommends that the Secretary of Defense direct
the appropriate DOD organizations to establish a deadline by which it intends to complete
the integration of the repositories and validate the completeness and reliability of
information.

DoD RESPONSE: Concur.

2

As indicated in the draft report, DoD has been working to better integrate the information technology budget and information technology systems inventory data through a variety of means. An automated process will be put in place over the next 24 months to ensure the common data in the two repositories is reconciled and accurate; to include clear identification of the number of Defense Business Systems. The Department is planning iterative steps to integrate the Select & Native Programming-Information Technology (SNaP-IT) budget database and Defense Information Technology Portfolio Repository (DITPR) systems inventory database. The initial increment, planned for completion by April 1, 2013, will ensure the appropriate association between budget investments and the systems inventory. Increment 2, planned for completion by April 1, 2014, will reconcile and remove duplicative data between the two data sources, improving both completeness and reliability.

RECOMMENDATION 3: The GAO recommends that the Secretary of Defense ensure that the Deputy Secretary of Defense, as the department's Chief Management Officer, direct the Deputy Chief Management Officer to include in DOD's annual report to Congress on compliance with 10 U.S.C. Section 2222 of the Fiscal Year 2005 National Defense Authorization Act, the results of the department's BPR efforts. Among other things, the results should include the department's determination of the number of systems that have undergone material process changes, the number of interfaces eliminated as part of these efforts (i.e., by program, by name), and the status of its end-to-end business process reengineering efforts.

DoD RESPONSE: Concur.

The Department recommends that GAO clarify that information on Business Process Reengineering (BPR) status must come from the appropriate pre-certification authorities; specifically, it is important to note that BPR Assertion is no longer the DCMOs responsibility. With the passage of the 2012 National Defense Authorization Act, BPR authority now rests with the Service CMOs and defense agency directors and therefore it would be appropriate for the GAO to direct its recommendation to BPR owners.

RECOMMENDATION 4: The GAO recommends that the Secretary of Defense ensure that the Deputy Secretary of Defense, as the department's Chief Management Officer, direct the Deputy Chief Management Officer to include in DOD's annual report to Congress on compliance with 10 U.S.C. Section 2222 of the Fiscal Year 2005 National Defense Authorization Act, an update on the Office of the DCMO's progress towards filling staff positions and the impact of any unfilled positions on the ability of the office to conduct its work.

DoD RESPONSE: Non-concur.

3

The DoD nonconcurs with the recommendation made by the GAO to include in the annual Congressional Report on Defense Business Operations an update on the Office of the DCMO's progress towards filling staff positions and the impact of any unfilled positions on the ability of the office to conduct its work. The Department does not believe that the annual Congressional Report on Defense Business Operations is the appropriate communication mechanism but is happy to provide GAO with an update.

Appendix III: GAO Contact and Staff Acknowledgments

GAO Contact	Valerie C. Melvin, (202) 512-6304 or melvinv@gao.gov
Staff Acknowledgments	In addition to the individual named above, Neelaxi Lakhmani and Mark Bird, Assistant Directors; Debra Conner; Rebecca Eyler; Michael Holland; Anh Le; Donald Sebers; and Jennifer Stavros-Turner made key contributions to this report.

www.ingramcontent.com/pod-product-compliance
Lightning Source LLC
Chambersburg PA
CBHW080910290526
45795CB00007BA/2479